HELLO, WORDS!

THE WORLD OF WORDS AND PICTURES

illustrated by Danièle Schulthess

BARRON'S

New York • London • Toronto • Sydney

Hello, Words! offers children ages four and up a complete selection of illustrated subjects and locales drawn from today's dynamic world. At this age children want precise information and can begin to understand abstract ideas. Each two-page spread provides a rich vocabulary that can be approached on three levels:

• a full-page illustration to explore and discuss objects, places, and actions. Because the "big picture" is so full of detail, it provides a rich opportunity for the "see-and-say" approach to reading that children love.

• a brief, illustrated story to teach the subjects and objects in each lesson.

• individual, captioned illustrations related to the main theme. These do not always duplicate those in the full-page illustration but are intended to enrich the main theme.

These three complementary approaches can be adapted to suit the interests of the young reader. With this book, children can expand their understanding of the world and learn key words.

All inquiries should be addressed to:
Barron's Educational Series, Inc.
250 Wireless Boulevard
Hauppauge, New York 11788

Library of Congress Catalog Card No. 88-39256

International Standard Book No. 0-8120-5788-0

Library of Congress Cataloging-in-Publication Data

Hello, words!: the world of words and pictures/illustrated by Danièle Schulthess.
    p.   cm.
Translation of: *Allô les mots.*
    Summary: Captioned illustrations and key words provide an introduction to a variety
of places, objects, and experiences including such areas as the zoo, the farm, the airport,
seasons, and plants and animals.
    ISBN 0-8120-5788-0
    1. Vocabulary—Juvenile literature. [1. Vocabulary.]
I. Schulthess, Danièle. ill. II. Title.
PE1449.A46 1989
428.1—dc19
                                                          88-39256
                                                          CIP
                                                          AC

PRINTED IN HONG KONG

012 4900 987654321

HELLO, WORDS!

the editor thanks the teachers
who kindly collaborated
in the preparation of this book

HOME

sofa

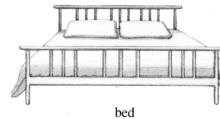
bed

Anthony and his Dad brush their teeth.

Mom hangs the clothes in the closet.

Charlotte carefully takes the cake she's baked out of the oven.

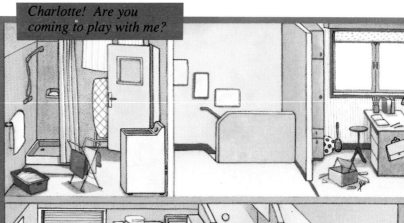

Charlotte! Are you coming to play with me?

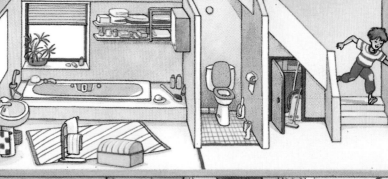

washing machine

refrigerator

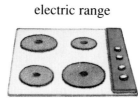

electric range

chair

stool

armchair

vase of flowers

lamp

television set

chest of drawers

Anthony sets the table—
forks on the left,
knives on the right.

Charlotte reads a magazine.
Anthony looks at the
comics.

Their mother puts a record
on the stereo turntable.

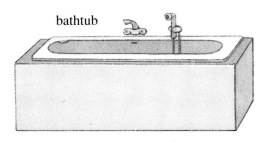
bathtub

towel rack

SCHOOL

tambourine

cymbals

dictionary

Today the class is going on a field trip.

The bus takes the children and teachers to the other end of town.

Is everyone here? Then we can go in.

This morning we will discuss the invention of the alphabet.

swimming pool

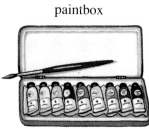
easel

paintbox

calculator

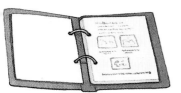
looseleaf notebook

pencil case

microcomputer

*Children, these knives and arrowheads
were made by Stone Age people.*

*My parents are geologists.
There are rocks all over our house!*

*Monkeys in the wild are much
more interesting than in the zoo!*

book bag

school books

gym bag

THE ATHLETIC FIELD

shoes with cleats

hurdle

bicycle

In the locker room, the students change their clothes. Some students take showers.

First, some stretching exercises to warm up.

Before the race, the runners put their feet against the starting blocks. Ready?

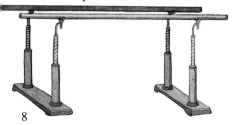

parallel bars

horse

glove, bat, and baseball

8

basketball hoop   for tennis   for Ping-Pong   barbells

racquets and balls

Ouch! Sometimes soccer can be a rough sport.

The winning volleyball team smiles for the cameras!

The winners get their medals. What a victory!

stopwatch

whistle

ice skate

football

TRANSPORTATION

ocean liner

bus

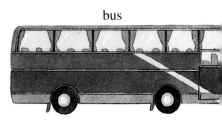

*The first humans
got around on foot.*

*Centuries later,
people rode horses.*

*The stagecoach was an early
means of group transportation.*

*When the light turns red, we
stop to let pedestrians cross.*

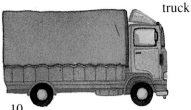

truck

plane

cross-country bike

trailer

helicopter

sailfish

train

The ancestors of today's cars and bicycles.

High-speed trains can go as fast as 180 miles per hour.

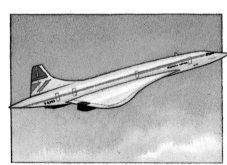

The supersonic Concorde flies from Paris to New York in less than four hours.

sailboat

car

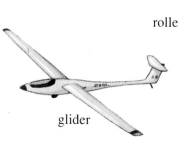
glider

roller skates

11

THE SERVICE STATION

gasoline pump

battery

tow truck

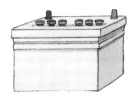
The children are fascinated by the car wash.

We're stopping at a service station. In the window, the children have seen a beautiful toy truck.

Mom said we can have it. Isn't that great?

The hood goes up and there's a little motor inside!

gasoline truck

steering wheel

squeegee and water bucket

wrench

tire

jack

oil can

hydraulic lift

You can clean the windshield, like they do at the service station.

You can even fill it up with gas from this tiny can.

The spare tire comes off, and the jack really lifts the toy truck.

automatic car wash

spark plug

windshield wiper

13

THE AMUSEMENT PARK

small boat

wheel of fortune

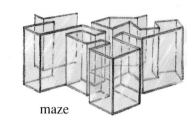

maze

The family goes to the amusement park. Anthony is thrilled!

*How about a ride on
the Ferris wheel?*

*We buy the tickets
and everyone takes a seat.*

*You have to fasten your seatbelt,
just like in an airplane!*

puppet show

the strongest man on earth!

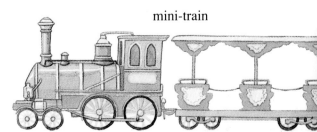

mini-train

14

bumper car

ride through the haunted house

Dad, look at that house!

*But Dad closes his eyes—
he's a little dizzy.*

*We're back on the ground. Now
shall we ride the scenic railway?*

wooden
horse

clown

enchanted cottage

15

THE CLOTHING STORE

scarf

gloves

hat

sweater

belt

Before you can make clothing, you have to draw a sketch.

Then you can take measurements on a form, and cut the pattern.

The pattern pieces are put together and sewn.

This winter, Charlotte will have a new jacket.

bathing suits

shorts

sun hat

T-shirt

sneakers

sweatshirt

pants

overalls

jacket

shirt

The designer chooses the fabric and the buttons.

The garment workers cut the fabric and sew it by machine.

At the fitting, last-minute alterations are made.
Could I wear it tonight?

ski jacket

boots

suspenders

socks

knee socks

17

THE SUPERMARKET

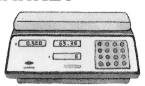
electronic scale

delivery cart

credit card

My favorite department is the bakery.

*You need flour to make bread—
lots of flour!*

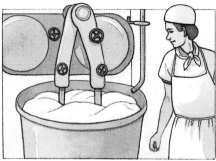
*The bread dough is kneaded
with huge beaters.*

*The loaves are cut
by machine.*

cash register

optical scanner

vending machine

basket

ug shampooer

shopping cart

hand truck

load

forklift

*Once it's shaped,
the bread is put into the oven.*

*The loaves are still warm.
The sliced bread is put into bags.*

*Whole wheat, rye, pumpernickel,
French, Italian, or pita . . .
What a choice!*

delivery truck

frozen foods

THE FARM

bale of hay

grains of wheat

ear of corn

barley

turnip

Everything is yellow and green!

The cows go into the barn.

Each one can eat
while it waits to be milked.

The farmer uses an
automatic milking machine.

harvester

milk can

bag of grain

bean plant

 tractor

 bags of fertilizer

 apple tree  apple

apricot tree  apricot

 silo

The milk is collected . . .
. . . while it is still warm.

It is skimmed, pasteurized,
and stored cold in tanks.

A truck comes to collect the milk,
which is later put into bottles or
cartons.

rabbit

hen   chick

duck

goose

21

THE SEASONS

rainbow

windmill

weather station

leaf buds

I love the countryside.
It's always changing.

On December 24th, at midnight, it's snowing in Paris.
The temperature is 32° F. (0° C.).

At the same time, in New York, it's seven PM on December 24th.
The temperature is 18° F. (-8° C.).

In Hong Kong, it's eight AM on December 25th.
It's 72° F. (22° C.).

Spring

Fall

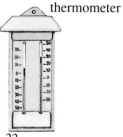
thermometer

rain gauge

cumulus clouds

cirrus clouds

leaf

mushroom

flower buds

acorns

Summer

In Moscow, it is two AM on December 25th.
The temperature is 18° F. (-8° C.).

In Australia, it's ten AM on December 25th.
The temperature is 68° F. (20° C.).

Winter

In Rio de Janeiro, it's nine PM. on December 24th.
The temperature is 80° F. (27° C.).

birds in a nest

mother and baby squirrels

stratus clouds

THE SEAPORT

buoy

salt ponds

pier

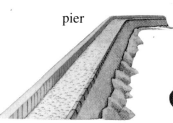
mussel

The harbor master is in charge of controlling ship traffic in the port.

The ship pulls up its anchor.

The pilot steers the ship.

When I grow up, I'm going to be a deep-sea diver.

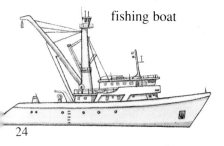
fishing boat

tub of fish

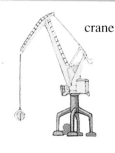
crane

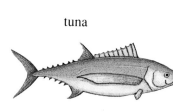
tuna

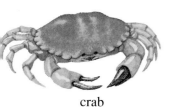
crab

black-headed gull

seaweed

sea gull

*The tanker is
filled with fuel oil.*

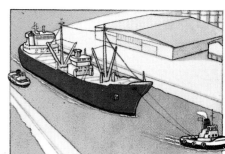
*A tugboat pulls the tanker
out of port.*

The tanker reaches the high seas.

red snapper

chart

diving equipment

THE MOUNTAINS

fir tree

woodchuck

mountain goat

The children are going to skiing school.

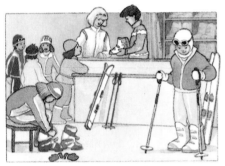

They try out their equipment: boot, skis, poles.

The instructor teaches them how to "snowplow."

Look! At last we can see the ski lodge.

eagle

hiking boots

backpack

trout

wild flowers

binoculars

snow partridge

*One by one, the skiers
go up the lift.*

*The snow-cleaning machine
clears a path.*

*The skis slide over the packed
powder. What a run!*

compass

canteen

pickax

PLANTS AND ANIMALS

wild ducks

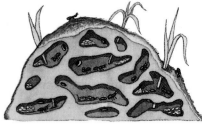
the inside of an anthill

At school, Charlotte loves to read books about nature.

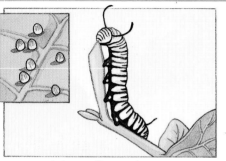
A butterfly egg bursts.
A caterpillar comes out.

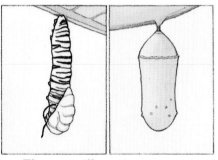
The caterpillar spins a cocoon
and becomes a pupa.

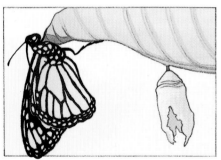
The cocoon opens.
The pupa has become
a beautiful butterfly!

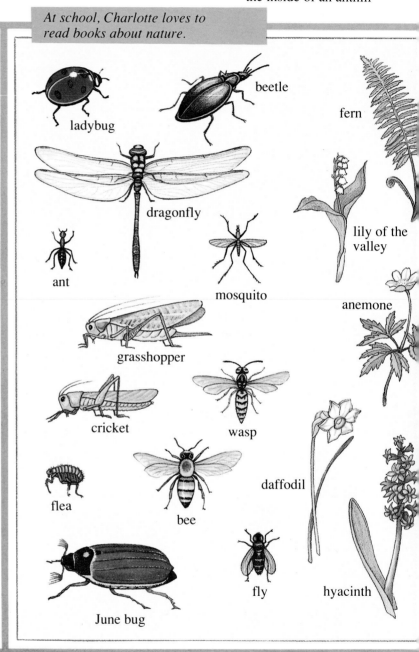

ladybug

beetle

fern

dragonfly

lily of the valley

ant

mosquito

anemone

grasshopper

cricket

wasp

daffodil

flea

bee

June bug

fly

hyacinth

heron's crest

bird's nest

pelican's beak

egg

daddy longlegs

feather

bluebell

stork nest

thistle

tulip

cactus

peony

mimosa

pigeon

nightingale

owl

pelican

robin

finch

lark

duck

swallow

black-headed gull

swan

hawk

penguin

The children want to see the flowers grow. They plant hyacinth bulbs.

They come to see them every day. Look, the stalks have pushed up out of the soil!

All the flowers have blossomed. Success!

honeycomb

poppy

iris

29

THE AIRPORT

control tower

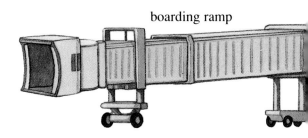

boarding ramp

These people are training for parachute jumping.

It's the day of their first jump! Everyone is suited up and ready to board the plane.

The plane has just taken off. Everyone's waiting for the big moment.

Charlotte is going to visit her grandparents.

fuel truck

baggage carrier

cargo lift

window

seat

food tray

This is it!
Free fall!

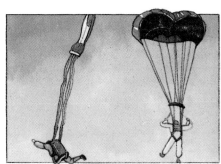

The parachutes open up
and fill with air.

The students make a soft landing.
Everyone is ready to try it again!

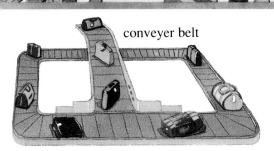

conveyer belt

automatic doors

THE CONQUEST OF SPACE

telescope

antenna

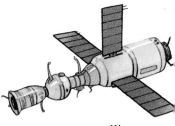
satellite

Will Charlotte and Anthony be able to go to the moon in the year 2000?

The lunar module separates from the space capsule.

The module hovers and lands gently on the moon.

The astronaut climbs down the ladder.

space suit

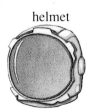
helmet

glove

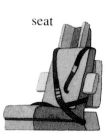
seat

food tray

32

launch pad

space probe

space pack

lunar vehicle

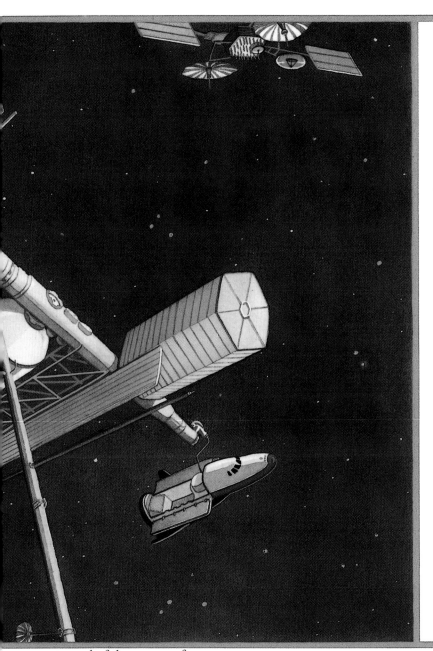

*For the first time
a person walks on the moon!*

*The instruments are set up.
One astronaut collects specimens.*

*On the moon, the force of gravity is
so weak that you can jump easily!*

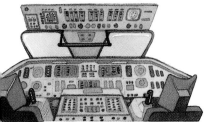

instrument panel of the spacecraft

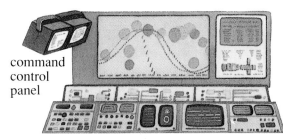

command
control
panel

MUSIC

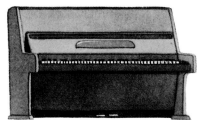

piano

drums

The musicians in the orchestra sit at their music stands.

They tune their instruments . . .

. . . and practice their music.

Everyone is here for the big music festival.

violin

harp

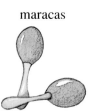

maracas

triangle

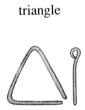

xylophone

saxophone

synthesizer

banjo

recorder

gong

The conductor bows.
The audience applauds.

Is everyone ready?
The conductor raises the baton . . .

. . . and the first notes
ring out in the concert hall.

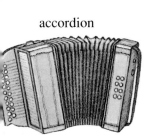
accordion

guitar

French horn

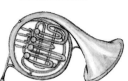

A TELEVISION BROADCAST

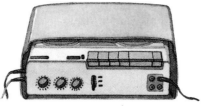
tape recorder

headphones

clock

The children are going to take part in a television broadcast.

The wardrobe mistress helps them to put on their costumes.

The hairdresser and makeup artist make them all look great.

The seven o'clock television newscast.
Quiet on the set: we're filming!

spotlights

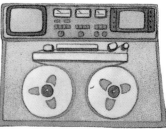
videotape recorder

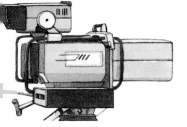
television camera

microphone

clapper boards

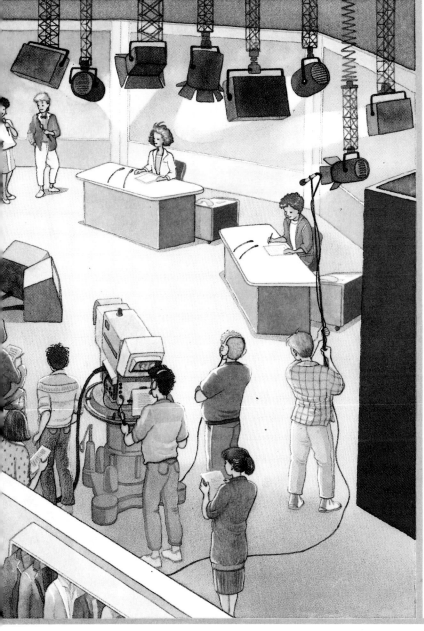

The children practice their lines before they go on the set.

At the signal, the camera begins filming the announcer.

The broadcast has begun. The children say their lines.

television monitor

mobile unit

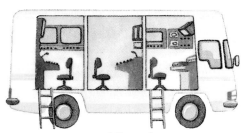

THE ZOO

crocodile

tiger

hippo

Lion cubs have just been born at the zoo.

The hungry lioness gets her dinner while the lion cubs nurse.

The zookeepers vaccinate a lion cub.

From her great height, the giraffe can see all her animal friends.

elephant

kangaroo

toucan

chimpanzee

rhinoceros

polar bear

penguin

deer

The zoo staff cleans the cages.

Visitors love to watch the lion cubs.

Here's the whole lion family. The lion plays with one of his cubs.

zebra

parrot

walrus

During her vacation,
Charlotte went to the seashore,
to the mountains,
and to a farm.

Look at all the pictures
and try to find the objects and animals
that she saw on each trip.

Which pictures show things
she wouldn't have seen?